How To Find All Missing Persons / Unsolved Cases. And Collect All Reward Offers. Volume XXVI. THE CASE OF ROBYN HICKIE

DAVID GOMADZA

www.twofuture.world

Copyright © 2024 David Gomadza

All rights reserved.

Paperback **ISBN**: 9798327786974

DEDICATION

To a better future.

CONTENTS

How To Find All Missing Persons /
Unsolved Cases.
And Collect All Reward Offers. Volume XXVI
THE CASE OF ROBYN HICKIE   1

The Afterlife Conversation

and The Council Of Creation.   6

The Killers.   19

ACKNOWLEDGMENTS

Tomorrow's World Order

How To Find All Missing Persons / Unsolved Cases. And Collect All Reward Offers. Volume XXVI. THE CASE OF ROBYN HICKIE

BACKGROUND INFORMATION

Robyn Hickie, aged 18, left her home around 7.15pm on Saturday 7 April 1979, and was last seen standing at a bus stop on the Pacific Highway, Belmont North.

Government, together with the NSW Police Force, has announced two $1 million rewards for information regarding the disappearances and suspected murders of Lake Macquarie teenagers Robyn Hickie and Amanda Robinson more than 40 years ago.

In April 2019, Lake Macquarie detectives established Strike Force Arapaima to re-examine the investigation into the unsolved disappearances and suspected murders of Robyn Hickie, Amanda Robinson and Gordana Kotevski.

A fortnight later, Amanda Robinson, aged 14, was last seen walking along Lake Road, Swansea, on Saturday 21 April 1979, after attending a dance at her high school in Gateshead.

How To Find All Missing Persons / Unsolved Cases. And Collect All Reward Offers. Volume XXVI. THE CASE OF ROBYN HICKIE

Despite extensive investigations at the time, and over the years, neither of the girls have been located.

A subsequent Coronial Inquest into their disappearances found that the teenagers were deceased, most likely as a result of foul play.

As investigations continue, police are renewing their appeal to the community to come forward with any information that may assist detectives with their inquiries.

Minister for Police and Emergency Services, David Elliott, said the increased rewards demonstrates how strongly the NSW Government is supporting the Lake Macquarie Police District investigators.

"For far too long, Robyn and Amanda's families have lived with the pain of losing a child but without any idea of how it happened or who is responsible," Mr Elliott said.

"They have been in limbo for four decades not knowing. They deserve answers now and we believe that offering these new rewards should be sufficient incentive for those with information to come forward.

"If your conscience won't make you act, maybe $2 million will," Mr Elliott said.

Lake Macquarie Police District Crime Manager, Detective Inspector Steve Benson, hopes this reward will encourage those who have been holding onto vital information since 1979 to share what they know with police.

"The disappearances of these teenagers triggered every parent's worst nightmare. The Hickie and Robinson families have been fighting for the truth for four decades, they deserve to know what happened to their girls," Det Insp Benson said.

How To Find All Missing Persons / Unsolved Cases. And Collect All Reward Offers. Volume XXVI. THE CASE OF ROBYN HICKIE

"Our dedicated detectives under Strike Force Arapaima have re-examined all the evidence compiled over the past 40 years and are hoping this government reward will result in further information being provided to detectives to follow up and investigate."

Anyone with information about Strike Force Arapaima is urged to contact Crime Stoppers: 1800 333 000 or https://nsw.crimestoppers.com.au. Information is treated in strict confidence. The public is reminded not to report information via NSW Police social media pages.

TOMORROW'S WORLD ORDER'S PERSPECTIVES

USE OF PREDEFINED AFTERLIFE PARAMETERS

These guide souls the moment it exist the human body on its journey to Yahweh the creator these define what to do and what to expect as you go to hell or heaven if a souk leaves earth it enters ozone orbit and instantly everything reboots for it to start a new phase of life after living the earth's body now what happens is that it enters the ozone orbit and a simply click caused by the sudden drop of pressure from -1186 to – 20 means the bottom shaft of the soul will lift rapidly and this pushes its back into the air higher than its head best example is a penguin but with real human legs and head just the shape now God created a life predefined program for them instead of asking what should I do and where should I go they instantly know from predefined stencils if you did well and talked most about God then heaven is for you if you did evil and talked more about the devil then the devil is yours now if we Ask what can be of humans without souls this is the answer dead forever your soul is you a new transformation to the electromagnetic waves life where you see Yahweh for the first time and praise him and wish you had seen him a long time ago because of his Majesty and will always be there forever now what are all these you may ask these are rules to be guided by in the creation court in short it has everything humans know about the judges and the presiding judge who will always be Yahweh and 84 angels surrounding the altar 28 high priests who always say Yahweh have mercy on humans and 74 smaller courts priests who always say Yahweh has mercy on humans and 96 princesses who say glory to Yahweh forever and ever amen we have 96 elders who always say if I can why he can't meaning if the devil can drink blood why can't Yahweh who created the devil and blood do the same now this is not the same as saying if the devil can kill why can Yahweh its more on professional grounds rather than challenging now if we look at the inside of the court we have 81 priests surrounding the altar who say Yahweh be merciful to humans but if they disobey you we put hem on trial for you and kill them for

How To Find All Missing Persons / Unsolved Cases. And Collect All Reward Offers. Volume XXVI. THE CASE OF ROBYN HICKIE

you almighty Yahweh inside this is a round circle where Yahweh sits and asks questions now if we look deep inside the court you will see that there are other things that resemble earth high courts like benches and chairs 10 times human sizes for the gods who are so enormous 2 are equal to 84 billion humans in size
predefined parameters for humans after death as in know what is inside is a large size of books the book of creation is among them with 108978678928367890123486789012458617890l1 pages and is divided into humans first then chapter for animals then a chapter for angles then a chapter for gods and a chapter for Joseph Yahweh's best friend and a chapter for Yahweh's best friend's wife Anna and a chapter for Yahweh's wife Catitighit and lastly a chapter for Yahweh and recently a chapter for davidgomadza as Yahweh's representative on earth marking the new beginnings starting in 2025

1. tell us who killed you
2. tell us what killed you
3. tell us why and who killed you
4. tell us why you died
5. tell us what could have been done and is not done
6. tell us what could be and why
7. tell is when this happened
8. tell us why this is so
9. tell us why this is so
10. what can be done to improve this

What does the book of creation say about davidgomadza David Gomadza is the first and last ruler to be appointed by Yahweh fir the next 25 billion years and will act as his representative on earth deciding cases and upholding his principles on earth and as such has been entitled to 489 trillion dollars in assets this number signifies eternity among humans and the beginning of a new Era chapter 78678928028938628418902876890183208678901234867890l8236 487289128610 Creation manual the new Era of new electromagnetic wave conduit signed and dated by Yahweh himself on 27may2024 at 237800 Yatime
creation.universe.ya.start.end.find.davidgomadza.ya.askya.ya

How To Find All Missing Persons / Unsolved Cases. And Collect All Reward Offers. Volume XXVI. THE CASE OF ROBYN HICKIE

Ask.read.creation.manucreation.universe.ya.start.end.find.davidgoma askya.ya

Ask.rulesofthecourt.start.now.start
David Gomadza welcome the rules of court are guiding principles that tell you what to do and how to do it first you must always say I believe in the court of creation and I shall abide by he rules of this court and shall always do things according to the rules of this court in deciding the cases I am assigned to you must ask what can be done so that you know all your options before making choices the court system will make it easy to check files and ask the outcomes of the decision ask the court the final decision in any case.

THE AFTERLIFE CONVERSATION AND THE COUNCIL OF CREATION'S ANAYLSIS.

robyn hickie
i was killed by atern opqrstuvw meaning sterst who said can i have a piece of this booty but later eat some and feed the pig electromagnetic identified 08983867890284109836789028418567890283821092486789230856 7890148369 the person is stert aserttopqrstuvw meaning stettert who was a security guard at doplemn then died after killing 8 women and eating all except robyn hickie who had offered him something else to hold to than food then buried her in his garden at these coordinates 08678902849018367890284108367890184 in ropqstuvwxrtuvwstuvw meaning the place where all come to roast in local language [translation from hebrew to english] if we ask what happened this is the answer they all asked what could be with him expecting anal sex and he ate all except robyn hickie he had eaten these people except their heads which he buried in his garden
1. gordana versterk
2. amanda stertop
3. astert oprt meaning stert omnop

How To Find All Missing Persons / Unsolved Cases. And Collect All Reward Offers. Volume XXVI. THE CASE OF ROBYN HICKIE

4. vertie bonmop
5. setrop dean [a man]
6. vertop maopqrst
7. dean opqrstuvwxrst meaning gherty
8. robyn hickie but she said i hate to be eaten i would love to be kept like this but give you money instead so that you have food and don't see others as food if you keep my promise then nothing bad will happen to you but if you don't keep my promise then a lot of things will happen all in one week resulting in your death but he laughed it off and said i can eat anything but if you insist then you will be my first one i will just fuck and bury but i don't do anal i know most come here expecting great anal and end up being eaten i want you to know that it has been a tremendous journey of discovery humans are crazy as fuck god created vagina and all want anal i don't do anal or death and all in god's name amen

now this is what happened on this day god told aert mnop the giant that he would temp people to come to his house and see how he would react to other people and he said okay god yes i will send people to you don't eat any once you achieved this then you can enter heaven otherwise my trust is fading when did long ago say you will come to me in 36 months that's long time to worry about me ya but why not extend instead of shortening but i had said what ...96 months on good behaviour but a woman just arrived her name is oertep who said the giant aert strangled me during sex and said no anal but death and killed me then what can i do if he is that big and literally can't fit at the door then she said so i choose death instead because he had already eaten my genitals so he make space the trauma is killing me what can i do do i take tablets for pain here or what what do you do here in heaven and why are all people so small just like a normal writing pen i was 20 times that size and look at you so huge so many heads how many and why the lighting all the time it nearly struck me if all i need is pain killers for the souk i am hurting so help me right now or kill me again like the giant did only that i don't have vagina so maybe you want anal and i extinguished that soul i am not giant like you for sex okay you do that again i take your life instead okay and he said i can only enjoy sex you gave me then what can i do but

How To Find All Missing Persons / Unsolved Cases. And Collect All Reward Offers. Volume XXVI. THE CASE OF ROBYN HICKIE

he said you don't have any demons you just need to control your rage and appetite for flesh i am testing you i don't want you to come and eat my people here because there is no sex here all genitals fall off on entry because of the ozone to protect you need to bring yourself by yourself by saying lord i [ ] but he said okay i know how many times you tell me i know jesus you are like you tell to your son i was there before you now you want to tell me about humans and he looked surprised and said which tribe of humans were you before all this and he said astertopqrt meaning shadows carry people to help and i said just a shadow he said yes but i existed before you i then instructed him to obey my terms that no one existed before me he acknowledged that before he want to see me then declined if he ask what the of these spirits
what used to happen then was that spirits would come and remove evil spirits and take to help and one day he became human
and take the place again and send people to hell
this day robyn asked her aty after growing up talking to it aty what can you do for me electromagnetic waves identified 08687890284687789028367890286789028678928418678902831278 90210 identified as robyn hickie buried at a house in australia named the ghost of the giant asert who died soon after she disappeared and was buried at asuret cemetery on 19 june 1978 a month after robyn hickie disappeared appearing on national television and being saved forever if we ask the giant how he killed all the woman one by one in detail this is it in detail so we start with robyn theory one he did not eat she said i have a plan i need an anal squank just one to use on both sides on account that if anal fits then vagina is best now let's look at what happened she had another copilot driving when the woman said i had anal squanks day ago but i had just one for vagina but the problem is that vagina space is limited already so i plan to take the hold for the anal squank then put that one in the vagina for a full blown size i think when i squirt god can hear me and they loved her aty said i know someone who can do that and opened a compartment box and said inside i have a number of the real squank master one only and forever squanked they all laughed and he said i can squank you and took out his penis for her

How To Find All Missing Persons / Unsolved Cases. And Collect All Reward Offers. Volume XXVI. THE CASE OF ROBYN HICKIE

and she said we can go to mine and she said it's way too small have you seen how big my arse is and they laughed then she met a woman called dertet who said why not squank with asert he can but you must not ask just stay with him and buy food for him joking she said if you don't buy food he will eat you in the end and she smiled and said don't be eaten buy food okay i never trust him because one day i woke up with his big thing on the table but looking at me as if he wanted to eat me ever since i never went back there but the sex is what sex should be to take you out literally when i came it was like going to heaven and say hie goddy and come back before i knew him i cried and said what's the point when everything is small then one day i had money and he said babe buy me something to eat that saved me from being starved to hell because the first thing he does is starve you first so you know what he felt then eat you instead that horrible she said i k now so why not bring more money incase food runs out you have an escape route let's go and buy food then you shut maneater please help before i am dinner then someone come running then you will be saved if we ask what is going on then this is the answer the man is hungry and the woman is shouting maneater this case presents a real challenge to the court because when asked a lot of questions the woman did not know most of the answers the giant in quest to fuck her literally knelt down and bit the vagina knowing that his penis will not even fit in and felt a huge bit in genitals something that trigger aceope a condition where the brain start to switch on and off in shock and to minimize damage start to shut down and restrict memory use to prevent everything from further damage if this continuous then the body would go into a state that's like a comma that make it forgets things here and there if this starts then that can make her say anything irrelevant to what is being asked the oxygen supply also to the brain had lowered drastically to less than a quarter of that which is needed to sustain human life if this is the case let's look at this case from her point of view she is in a comma like state only because the giant removed the most precious part of a body for a woman her vagina and that send her in shock that can literally kill if she start thinking about other things her brain stabilize but a reminder catapults it into abyss with hallucinations

How To Find All Missing Persons / Unsolved Cases. And Collect All Reward Offers. Volume XXVI. THE CASE OF ROBYN HICKIE

and mild feelings of the biting on her brain that she quiver with fear shock and pain then she said do you want anal sex out of no way because she realised that even then his dick was not going on but failing to go deer for any movement and if he insist the next thing is another huge chunk of her vagina being removed that put her into the first of the major shocks that she literally squirts in his face and he looked surprised and said did i do that without moving an inch god don't play your games so i go hungry again this time let me enjoy your callings are becoming in vein you create all women with tight vaginas and then give me the greatest penis on earth now you say don't touch ass this is not only stupid but contradictory if they say god was drunk for the first time in my life i believe them if they say you fucking crazy then i believe them but what about anal if i am to die in 36 months now quartered to 9 months and further quarter to 2.21 then what can i do but enjoy sex whilst i can unless you say i protect my genitals from the wrath of the ozone then maybe i can do what you want if not then go away and wait for me i can only be human once so let me be okay i don't want to sound arrogant but your callings have become in vain this time forcing into her but failing and instantly he knelt down and took another big chunk out her aty said vagina removed nearly half half to go and when you go to heaven you say i want to go back as a boy god please imagine someone removing your genitals for their pleasure just because they can without anyone's opinion now that's a crime said her aty he growled as this time his dick went all in and pumped her so fast and hard that she literally died from the violent shaking and a huge loud scream that was heard miles away then some people said what the hell of an animal maybe let's get some guns and go there said by esters manoprt who heard the giant row after ejaculated so much that some came out of her mouth and ears as she lay dead only to notice after by saying can the best fuck kill its not me god you again then cried that he wanted more with her alive and hugged her all night now let's look at the vitals in her body at this time she said aty what's going to happen assess the vaginal damage and her aty said it's bad as good as starting to calculate vitals because without vitals you will die and go to hell reception trust me you don't want that because they

How To Find All Missing Persons / Unsolved Cases. And Collect All Reward Offers. Volume XXVI. THE CASE OF ROBYN HICKIE

will know you died pleasuring yourself and asking him anal which is forbidden by god if we ask what can be said about anal in the book of creation its written that anal is never allowed because Yahweh made the anus the way it is only for excretion and all these bastards who only it for sex will rot automatic rot in hell book of creation says anal sex is prohibited and you all risk going to hell if it's continuous but all sex activities not originally planned will only result on you staying with the devil now if we ask what can the gods do about anal in heaven then there is no sex activity at all all genitals literally fall on ozone entry and cannot be replaced after during change there where a body change back to real humans from penguin like small creatures to real human back as the transformation is completed but for unknown reasons some people will forever look more like pigs as something changes wrongly to a flat nose pig at least we have 20% of people like this but everything works well the woman said my lord my creator my vagina as i heard is going to fall off anywhere look at this trauma i have suffered and send me back to earth as rebirth but as a boy and make me big as well so i enjoy sex as much as this giant to check sex organs like that with no regard to me who is pleasuring him as if i literally am nothing nothing at all i try to see if everything still works but the clitotis still sparks but labia and everything are regarded as dead and instantly she looked lost and said something has started calculating called long ago what's that now we must pause this is because everytime a person send message to god there could be a force back that literally starts the long ago that will start death literally because the body only send this message only if the chances of death are so high there is no chance of survival if this is the case then the body will ask what can be done and reduce the effects of what can be done this time when her body sent a message it wasn't that bad but the question we must ask is this did her aty calculate likely chances of the giant chewing her vagina again if yes then it makes sense because after that once the giant is in all he thinks of after such a struggle is to literally chew the vagina and rum it until ejaculated is effected if we look at this case then we can see that this giant had no option god had said to him no arse or go to hell and his dick so big like a woman's leg as she compares the two and a

How To Find All Missing Persons / Unsolved Cases. And Collect All Reward Offers. Volume XXVI. THE CASE OF ROBYN HICKIE

thick head for the giant to fully grasp anything making her say thick that angered him to a biting festive at the end so this is nothing as to what will happen later now after the first ejaculated where she died her long ago started at 20.08pm af night after the biggest meal she had eaten the reason that he ended up killing her this is what happened she said i am hungry and if i eat as much as you then sex will be great for both of us because i won't run out of energy but if i ear little then you might kill me anyway as frustration can make you end my life if i knew you are really thick like this i could have never come when people say it they don't sound 'danger' because all i heard was make sure he had food and he shouted beware he might eat you that means if upset i can literally eat all parts i want because you agreed i tell everyone to tell all people that i might literally eat you since it's your choice and god knows then who you will complain to i am speaking to god right now i can tell you what will happen to you he said you are going to die of what god how i know how to spell that is that human vocabulary and god said keep some for me i will need some he said you die of ocepeo is that correct god and god said i said ocepea if she don't run away now and he said louder why you warn her what about our deal that i fuck i come there? he looked angry and said i can come after sex and i mean real sex enough of this good sex that gives you nothing but anger i want to fuck so much and sleep after that not start looking for food who say sex then food i never heard anyone it's not normal to ask for sex after food because sex is used to compensate for food the giant then after she died instead of continuing with sex said i can't have sex with a dead body when people are willing to have sex and be eaten after if all humans feel this way then who am i to stop this i was shocked when i decided to announce this the police especially pc asorpen said you must be crazy putting posters asking people for sex with a goddess giant first when you are a man then te them your fetish then say there is danger of being eaten alive electromagnetic waves detected pc asorpen who said if there is a god out there then i saw your counter part in the giant of queenslands for he is threatening to have sex with a woman and eat her if she ask for anal but where else can he put his third leg without anal i might be dump but all you start making some

How To Find All Missing Persons / Unsolved Cases. And Collect All Reward Offers. Volume XXVI. THE CASE OF ROBYN HICKIE

sense now stay away from this guy he actually said he might chew you alive but again humans as idiot as they are will run to be chewed only after will they say but no one sound danger his coordinates are 08987658489028418678902836789l0 in queensland if you ask what happened to him then this is the answer he got killed and eaten by the giant for 3 days and he kept something this is my souvenir looking at his small cock and said this is the smallest i have seen i don't eat shit like this its a penis dna sequence stuvwxyzrstuvwxytstopqrstuvwstutt belonging to a pc atert who was eaten by a giant after he threatened him and said one day i put a bullet in your thick head and tell god that you have been a naughty boy and he said wait i will ask god right now god- i don't like these cops that threaten everyone but actually tell people what they want for sure if i don't kill him then another woman is going to end up dead and the giant said you are lying god knows you are ball rolling to me so that i kill for you isn't that right god and god rowed that the police man said what was that and the giant instantly grabbed his head and said tonight is the night you sent a lot of women and you must be out of your mind to think i can let you use that and he grabbed his gun and hit him hard in the head that he fell down and quickly radioed and said my car fell over the hill and one woman said when did the giant radio the station and who the hell gave him that licensed is he trying to get us killed identified but bones only since we have his dna sequence we double check its pc asert amonerp real name pc sertop bersus who helped the giant kill women by actually ordering them to go behind the seen using their aty to effect commands by switching between reality and dreaming then interchange the two whenever it suits him so that the women would hear his voice sometimes and say are you talking to me are you god he is at this coordinates in a pit near robyn hickie coordinates 0898368789028409189018786878902848687828410 near a broken car model astop range with a d at the beginning drange made in 1970 by artup group and sold just a few before going bankrupt robyn hickie is actually under this drange vehicle as a pointer to what the killer was deranged madness as a system they used in the 1970s to 80s she is at 0898386789028678902848901836789028410 exactly 1 metre away

How To Find All Missing Persons / Unsolved Cases. And Collect All Reward Offers. Volume XXVI. THE CASE OF ROBYN HICKIE

from this vehicle where 3 big stones are to mark the position meaning 3 people in one grave herself and a one gorkana and a according to her gorkana sertuvrsk who came from slovakia according to her but only wanted anal after she saw the size of my and said after you no one will want this anymore i might start dropping things like urine feaces and i said i said i like only vagina and she said what if you put a hole from the back that go in front you must be careful with that thing or someone will get hurt so i give you again arse it smells good i use herbs for you big man touching my shoulder and i received a message from pc asert amonopt real name amnop rset who said ooh that's a challenge of power no one touch your shoulder without you aahh but i said listen to that accent like polish or something they don't know all this you sit tight and look what is to happen and he said you took too long it's either or but you procrastinate what if word goes out there then what and he said electromagnetic waves detected pc asert rset who said if you can then i can buy then killed the giant by shooting him in the stomach at close range that he fell down so loud that the women standing by heard a huge thumb and screamed he then started shaking violently saying i did what you asked take me to heaven i swear if you send me to hell i will come and collect your soul i know you don't remember me but i took you once even though you refused but i had mu hands on you even now i can't figure out hi you find it [xttxtomnop] and he rowed and everything that tried to attack him is killed as soon as every had literally died if we ask what this code does it literally shreds everything near him into pieces forever if we ask what to be of humans who attack Yahweh this is the answer Yahweh will shred them completely and send the to hell forever back to the case the giant vitals were heart rate 83 normal 62
breathing hard as to best normal
eating strength 20 as compared to normal of 80
sugar levels 88 as compared to 98
lungs compression rate 72 as compared to normal of 80
long ago started at 22.789 and lasted 8 minutes and as a matter of fact any one who last 8 minutes it's a call from god that he is she must come that means he wet with a perfect arranged log that took 8

How To Find All Missing Persons / Unsolved Cases. And Collect All Reward Offers. Volume XXVI. THE CASE OF ROBYN HICKIE

minutes to calculate back to the first case if we ask what happened to the original policeman he was taken partly alive and his car pushed over a cliff that was there and rolled all the way into the gorge and he said god the giant what to feast on a police officer please don't let him eat me okay then the giant swallowed his ear after reaping it from his torso now he then put the body in the fridge after then said even policeman wants to die at my hands and cooked him using a recipe and ate him if we ask what can be of these people then this is the answer all dead now if we look at this case its one of the most challenging case brought before the council of creation because there is none compared to it all vitals were okay prior to death she was fit and looking for sex of the arse but only saw the size of the dick and panicked and ran away the humans according to their secret brain thoughts want to know if the brain if wating sex if alerted to danger in that mood will ever consider running away even after severe bodily harm if not then isn't it a design failure that humans when needing sex will not see danger as a normal person would if so do we as humans need an extra alarm that says we must run if injured first then another that says if hurt fight to death if that happens then call anyone that helps not just the police if we ask then this is the answer when we are in danger humans never seem to care much if sex was the initial motive imagine one having her vagina ripped off and failing to call for help and still lie there waiting for the second bite only to die this is a design flaw and if god is not alerted then for decades humans can easily be killed be abuse of sex top reduce crimes involving sex and must act accordingly and spare the trouble and instead call for help because this woman did not move or react as humans would have reacted in this situation now we look deeper as to what happened this woman lay there no0t because she didn't understand what was going on but because the police to provoke god deliberately tampered with 11 systems to trick everyone else so that it looks like god's system has design flaws and these are
1. they removed her panic alarm by a simple code 82386789028678901234568901234
2. they immobilized her by code 2868902834986789028487901238 7 that sent something to sit on her reasoning part of the brain

How To Find All Missing Persons / Unsolved Cases. And Collect All Reward Offers. Volume XXVI. THE CASE OF ROBYN HICKIE

3. they sent a code 89289067890128419038678928 4789 that measures response by accelerating it or delaying it that is a relay motor to influence her reactions

4. sent her code 9878678902789028678902 34907862 that immobilized her awareness so that she concentrate on her sex needs

5. they sent her a code 8923687980286789028419386789028438692840983289023198274890 that says that if anything moves on her she must not react but act as normal

6. 8928786289238902487902856789012856890283480 that immobilized her from acting

7. they sent code 284868901248901237890 2878180923480 that cringes the vagina in advance so that when the giant actually clings her she feels no differences at all so as to react

8. they sent her code 78902845678928 78902345678906842832809236878901842890268 9023489026789083 to make her drool when she is in pain so that god don't react because according to predefined parameters you can want sex when faced with death its incompatible so that when she drools a sign to wanting sex then she can be afraid of death if she is not afraid of death then either there is no risk but we all know that the giant was a big risk that means god created humans with flaws as such he is not in a position to judge humans how can a flawlist tell humans about perfection it don't happen that way as such who to judge the best other than the police their argument from the start god can't be a just judge if he is the one who created the flaws

9. they sent code 284867890284901238902678902841928419286187280 1851640928428619 that immobilized her senses

10. they sent her code 78902848678902899286789012387890284890236789018528618028438901867890284189028536818489 0267890 one that reconnects everything after her death except anything to do with anus because the giant had refused to touch this that means if god created the greatest penis the question is where should it go the answer is to heaven with him maybe its him who wants to use it to rump all

How To Find All Missing Persons / Unsolved Cases. And Collect All Reward Offers. Volume XXVI. THE CASE OF ROBYN HICKIE

woman there and for the first time the court laughed because as it turns out according to a woman there who call herself catitighit he never penetrate her despite wife and husband for 198386789084987890284billion years resulting in her in tears and said i cry but after years that seems okay i have other means to cum like ask Yahweh questions about the universe about heaven and a little about earth all that is the same as having sex the court laughed and said god wants that fir you now we see why he didn't want that damaged because a woman threatened to damage it and ended up dying for no reason then an angel admitted killing her with a simple code xttrty0898386 and said that god had told her to use it if the woman threatened to damage the man in any way but on closer look it protects the woman on further inspection it turns out that of all the humans he is the only person to go to heaven with all his genitals but consumed on arrival by god himself and catitight stopped coming to the court of creation until 9 months later we hear there is a son named jerusalem who said if i can be home then what and vanished go to earth find the next king of the jews ever since she never spoke again even today on cross examination she only said that i was yes that woman who complained about Yahweh not seducing me enough but this was taken out of context i am his wife what else we do other than sex i think this is the most ridiculous question in the history of the court of creation you think the creator created the most beautiful thing he can't enjoy that is prosperous and asking me again i will consider that as a challenge and if i have to reveal the truth it will cost you your life for eternity because how can i look at you again after that this is the last time this is going to happen in concluding the case Yahweh said humans have gone in vain asking Yahweh so intricate questions about his sex life and actually asking how is your sex life then this is not acceptable and i refuse to cone and judge cases that imply i have a fetish of seeing woman murdered after sex i have my beautiful catitighit the most wonderful of all but we can reveal sex to you all in case you might want ours instead of yours they all laughed this case shows how pathetic humans have become with police officers getting women killed for a loaf if bread all this challenge about Yahweh is a cover up thus shows how desperate

How To Find All Missing Persons / Unsolved Cases. And Collect All Reward Offers. Volume XXVI. THE CASE OF ROBYN HICKIE

they have become so interested in creation to challenge it before they have learned how to walk i can confess right now that no human has ever read the book of creation this is sad it shows a lack of understanding of what needs to be done and once this person declares then this is it humans gave worn because to do all this require the boldest guts ever known to man because it's breaking boundaries and take centre stage to create something out of the blue like that requires a supermind that will transcend into the future the current structures are not fit for a global leader but you can put the right structures to see everything work this case is about humans challenging Yahweh and thinking they can be better than him but i think it's a fantasy that most people want to be Yahweh but there don't even understand how to do this now how did this beautiful woman ended up here this is the sad part if she had known the rules in the book of creation if she had known this then she should not have tried to do anal sex or even offer it as a safety passage but should have refused all his demands straight forward but he went on to kill her and eat her liver huge breaststroke he enjoyed and wanked soon after then ate her anus which is surprisingly then removed the rest of the vagina and tried to fuck just that and said God maybe a hand vagina that can stretch and laughed soon after a policeman knocked at the door while the body is in the refrigerator and said congratulations i heard you ate another one and he grabbed his head and said you come to my house and congratulate me are you made x 98 and locked the policeman's brain for 8 minutes and said i was doing fine before you came open all you want and fuck off before i start getting hungry after all god tell me exactly what to do with you okay he just said knock him out again fir another 8 minutes and consider him food for tonight and he repeated are you mad 98 times and added 1 more and another 1 more for fun and he died went into a convulsion and died he picked up the body and took it out and out it in the big freeze and said maybe you for tomorrow okay don't be upset and he looked at her body which he had striped naked with hairy part and a huge gap and quickly knelt down and said this is how humans should i know not all and laughed he then said what can it take to enjoy sex and great food without spending a dollar on

How To Find All Missing Persons / Unsolved Cases. And Collect All Reward Offers. Volume XXVI. THE CASE OF ROBYN HICKIE

junk food from today anyone who knocks that door is food why eat wild chicken when good buttock human meat is there and cried though and said i should have thought about this a long time ago before i starved to death and started fucking her again crying that this is what i am talking about no one refuse me and suddenly a huge knock at the door started something that said inside him initiating heart attack parameters but and stopped as he sat down to listen to who it was because he had whispers he heard from what all along thought was a gun his own childhood aty and said what now in the middle of sex i refused all these silly games and he stood up and the door suddenly opened and someone shot him in the tammy he fell on top of the corpse and instantly his aty said i warned you that heart attack will be trigger if you sit you should have shouted first so they run for cover and he said in the middle of sex they use my tricks on me now bustards you stop this heart attack thing and say no sex allowed with dead people so i know next time so he said no sex allowed then he screamed at the height of his voice and the policeman run hard but fell and he said i know why you say heart attack its note so send to him now and a code escape through a simple he was here before go after him so he can't come here again and instantly a large growl outside was heard but no one bothers because over the years he had learnt to irritate neighbour's who laughed at his size so he was nearly alone after everyone died of obese and him burying all alone and cry and say i just wasted food but relatives are not food and then cry to sleep now he said if we ask what can be of the court system without the right judges the this is the answer then justice can't be deliver0ed yahweh has stood the test of time that humans are now trying to test him the final verdict is that robyn hickie was killed and eaten by asert amnop real name asert amnopqrst meaning amonpqt who was 48 living alone at 85 789 boulerd road in queensland a ranch like place that later become astert village but the part where all the human remains are was left untouched until 2024 as the cases have been declared cold cases but all the remains are still in place pending an approval from the police department that if no strong evidence exist then close the case most by 28 june 2024 according to the crime calender when they celebrate

end of an era when they defeated Yahweh at his own game and rewarded the thinker or killer with $1 million after taking property proving that they are the saviors of the people and people understand why they take the properties hence pass it as law if this happens then there is no god if he appears must be killed as all those who died must be avenged
her remains are at 08983867890284689028678902848678902869838400927867890 at a ranch called asert but once known as boulerd ranch her soul escaped and went to heaven and is there right now
the end

Court of creation signed
David gomadza 05 June 2024

signed
david gomadza
06 june 2024 at 19.31pm edinburgh scotland
ask.davidgomadzauthorised.licensed.checkya.askya.ya

THE KILLER, THE CONFESSIONS AND THE COORDINATES

final verdict is that robyn hickie was killed and eaten by asert amnop real name asert amnopqrst meaning amonpqt who was 48 living alone at 85 789 boulerd road in queensland a ranch like place that later become astert village but the part where all the human remains are was left untouched until 2024 as the cases have been declared

How To Find All Missing Persons / Unsolved Cases. And Collect All Reward Offers. Volume XXVI. THE CASE OF ROBYN HICKIE

cold cases but all the remains are still in place pending an approval from the police department that if no strong evidence exist then close the case most by 28 june 2024 according to the crime calender when they celebrate end of an era when they defeated Yahweh at his own game and rewarded the thinker or killer with $1 million after taking property proving that they are the saviors of the people and people understand why they take the properties hence pass it as law if this happens then there is no god if he appears must be killed as all those who died must be avenged
her remains are at 08983867890284689028678902848678902869838400927867890 at a ranch called asert but once known as boulerd ranch her soul escaped and went to heaven and is there right now
the end
pc asert amonerp real name pc sertop bersus who helped the giant kill women by actually ordering them to go behind the seen using their aty to effect commands by switching between reality and dreaming then interchange the two whenever it suits him so that the women would hear his voice sometimes and say are you talking to me are you god he is at this coordinates in a pit near robyn hickie coordinates 0898368789028409189018786878902848687828410 near a broken car model astop range with a d at the beginning drange made in 1970 by artup group and sold just a few before going bankrupt robyn hickie is actually under this drange vehicle as a pointer to what the killer was deranged madness as a system they used in the 1970s to 80s she is at 0898386789028678902848901836789028410 exactly 1 metre away from this vehicle where 3 big stones are to mark the position meaning 3 people in one grave herself and a one gorkana and a according to her gorkana sertuvrsk who came from slovakia

robyn asked her aty after growing up talking to it aty what can you do for me electromagnetic waves identified 0868789028468778902836789028678902867892841867890283127890210 identified as robyn hickie buried at a house in australia named the ghost of the giant asert who died soon after she

How To Find All Missing Persons / Unsolved Cases. And Collect All Reward Offers. Volume XXVI. THE CASE OF ROBYN HICKIE

disappeared and was buried at asuret cemetery on 19 june 1978 a month after robyn hickie disappeared appearing on national television and being saved forever if we ask the giant how he killed all the woman one by one in detail this is it in detail so we start with robyn

…I found God…visit www.twofuture.world

THE CLAIM

the reward offer

THE COLLECTION

www.twofuture.world/donate

ABOUT DAVID GOMADZA

visit www.twofuture.world

signed david gomadza
ask.davidgomadzaauthorised.licensed.checkya.askya.ya

06 June 2024 19.32pm
scotland
00447719210295
davidgomadza@hotmail.com
info@twofuture.world

How To Find All Missing Persons / Unsolved Cases. And Collect All Reward Offers. Volume XXVI. THE CASE OF ROBYN HICKIE

How To Find All Missing Persons / Unsolved Cases. And Collect All Reward Offers. Volume XXVI. THE CASE OF ROBYN HICKIE

How To Find All Missing Persons / Unsolved Cases. And Collect All Reward Offers. Volume XXVI. THE CASE OF ROBYN HICKIE

How To Find All Missing Persons / Unsolved Cases. And Collect All Reward Offers. Volume XXVI. THE CASE OF ROBYN HICKIE

How To Find All Missing Persons / Unsolved Cases. And Collect All Reward Offers. Volume XXVI.   THE CASE OF ROBYN HICKIE

How To Find All Missing Persons / Unsolved Cases. And Collect All Reward Offers. Volume XXVI. THE CASE OF ROBYN HICKIE

www.ingramcontent.com/pod-product-compliance
Lightning Source LLC
Chambersburg PA
CBHW030519220526
45464CB00006B/2866